ENTWINED

Also by Carol Frost

Honeycomb (2010)

The Queen's Desertion (2006)

I Will Say Beauty (2003)

Love and Scorn: New and Selected Poems (2000)

Venus & Don Juan (1996)

Pure (1994)

Chimera (1990)

Day of the Body (1986)

The Fearful Child (1983)

Liar's Dice (1978)

The Salt Lesson (1976)

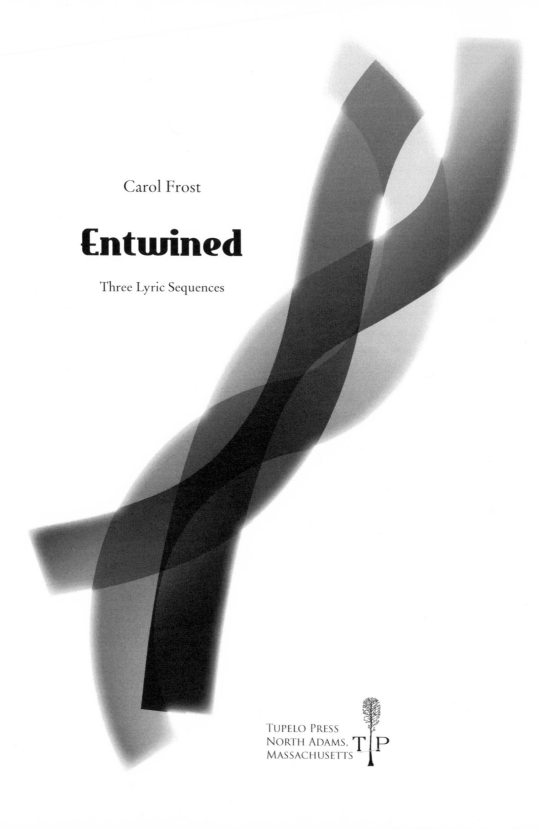

Carol Frost

Entwined

Three Lyric Sequences

TUPELO PRESS
NORTH ADAMS,
MASSACHUSETTS

Entwined
Copyright 2014 Carol Frost. All rights reserved.

Library of Congress Cataloging-in-Publication Data

Frost, Carol, 1948–
 [Poems. Selections]
 Entwined : three lyric sequences / Carol Frost. -- First paperback edition.
      pages cm
Includes bibliographical references.
ISBN 978-1-936797-49-3 (pbk. : alk. paper)
I. Title.
PS3556.R596A6 2014
811'.54--dc23
        2014026038

Cover and text designed by Bill Kuch. Composed in Stempel Garamond, Clearface, and East Market.
Cover photograph: Andrew Sprague (artinsur.blogspot.com).

First paperback edition: September 2014.

Certain of these poems first appeared in the books *Pure*, copyright © 1994 by Carol Frost; *Venus and Don Juan*, copyright © 1996 by Carol Frost; *Love and Scorn: New and Selected Poems*, copyright © 2000 by Carol Frost; *The Queen's Desertion*, copyright © 2006 by Carol Frost; *Honeycomb*, copyright © 2010 by Carol Frost; and/or in *American Poetry Review, The Atlantic Monthly, Gettysburg Review, Indiana Review, Kenyon Review, Missouri Review, New England Review, Ninth Letter, New Virginia Review, New York Times, North American Review, Partisan Review, Plume Poetry, Poetry, Poetry International, Prairie Schooner, Shenandoah, Smartish Pace, Southern Review, Subtropics, TriQuarterly, Virginia Quarterly Review*, and *Volt*.

Tupelo Press
P.O. Box 1767; 243 Union Street, Eclipse Mill, Loft 305
North Adams, Massachusetts 01247
Telephone: (413) 664–9611 / editor@tupelopress.org • www.tupelopress.org

Tupelo Press is an award-winning independent literary press that publishes fine fiction, nonfiction, and poetry in books that are a joy to hold as well as read. Tupelo Press is a registered 501(c)(3) nonprofit organization, and we rely on public support to carry out our mission of publishing extraordinary work that may be outside the realm of large commercial publishers. Financial donations are welcome and are tax deductible.

ART WORKS.
arts.gov

Supported in part by an award from the National Endowment for the Arts

for Luca, Marco, and Zoë

Contents

II
Abstractions (1991–2000)

III
Apiary Poems (2004–2011)

Lucifer in Florida

I Lucifer, cast down from heaven's city which is the stars,
soar darkly nights across the water to islands
and their runway lights — after sunset burning petals;
sights, sorrows, all evils become the prolonged shadows
and lightning through palm trees and the ancient oaks.
. . . And ride with darkness, dark below dark, uttermost
as when the cormorant dives and the fish dies, eye-deep
in hell; the bird is I, I hide in its black shining
spread of wings raised drying afterward on a tree bough.
Nothing more onyx or gold than my dark wings.
Yet Venus rising, the off chords and tender tones
of morning birds among the almonds, small flames
of lemon flowers, phosphorus on the ocean,
all I've scorned, all this lasts whether I leave or come.
The garden fails but the earth's garden lives on
unbearable — elusive scent on scent from jasmine
mixed with brine, the smell of marshes, smells of skin
of fishermen, burned rose and a little heroic
while leviathan winds rise and darkness descends.
Sin and death stay near, black with serenity,
calm in dawn's light suggestions. If the future is
a story of pandemonium, perfection's close —
from the sea the islands at night, from the island
the sea at night with no lights rest equally, lit by
a wanderer's memory bringing dark and light to life,
luminous and far as dreams endure, charcoal and flame
in a fire, the embers of pride and pain in each breath.

I

Voyage to Black Point

~

Midway on our life's journey, I found myself
In dark woods, the right road lost.
— Dante

For I would travel without wind or sail,
And so, to lift sorrows from my mind,
Let your memories of sea-days long fled
Pass over my spirit like an outspread sail.

What have you seen?

"We have seen lost sea-beaches,
And waves and stars and known many wars."
— Baudelaire

The Poet's Black Drum

Come in the silent acting in a dream now wayfarer

come back from that deepest paradise

where all that haven't breath the breathless mouth

may summon: Tell us all about your journey fishing::

barbels: stony teeth in the throat: aching shoulders:

and what Florida locals call tailing (the drifting fleece)—

drum underneath the flutter—: fecund

with slender parasites: beauty's flesh::

Black Point

I want to say oracle: sea grass: crab cluck:

swollen sheepshead in a fitful sea nodding assent::

I who listened for decades to familiar voicings

now heard Delphic imaginings low and sweet:

hallucinogenic as when the dolphin crests

in early morning vapor and light mixing on water

the leap and splash thunderous: a flight of birds:

one piping: syrinx in the wind: a rising sea—

woman behind the bank of ice who says

no crabs today: hours in a small boat

I converse with sea meadows

fish human nature: look and remember::

the zigzag to Black Point: Corycian Cove:

with my questions: alone suddenly

in panic—luminous neck of a snake

become a turtle: black and white tattered fish—

then the sort of trance: beneath sense some

early rune: I've traveled to hear this sound.

Blue Crab

A rearing up: the pincers waved in air: By God you better let me be:

brine bubbled at the mouth: bent foam and current having laved the shell:

water shouldering: Saturnal: deranged in the wire trap—

an inverted funnel like a halved hourglass—: ten legs makeshift on land::

How far its life reaches in the argosy beneath the surface of the sea: what I

ask: when emotion wakens: Calli: beautiful; nectes: swimmer::

To tumble down layers of sense into the warring gardens:

only to eat to molt to procreate: salt sea mud breeding in the shoals.

And then to come back, as from a museum: Goya barely bearable:

or from Medea's grave mind:: a taste of salt air:: I take up the crab in tongs.

Sandpiper

Pillar of salt then the spell reversed: vowels

moistened in the mouth: tone of hurry::

in the distance weird bubbling whistle

bububu-hLeeyooo: Febru Febr-uary ooo:

how it is to be that happy and afraid:

now here alone rocking on the winter wave

hull dead bumping the shoal: wrists cold:

casting reeling in mind cold nothing not

for days: palm roots hold more movement:

until like Euridyce's head and shoulders come

into view something stirs water pearls on the line

fish nudging: I could weep for joy.

Dolphin

A slow storm coming across the gulf:

a raddling: wind in palmettos? or a gaunt bird's bill?

Given ears and skin and eyes nose and tongue: given stories

of arrival—the perfect birth, Alexander's tide, Caesar's—

oh yearn fear portend contrive praise deny but not abstract::

I've seen the reddened knees of students in winter,

in shorts when there was merely a slant of cold sun

and once tentacle burns across the chest of a dead tourist—

how blue the sea is, box jelly fish too few and small

to matter. Neurotoxins, pfff. I'm . . . —Well::

On leeward mangrove branches herons egrets:

yellow tridents rumbling far far away: on the horizon

a small bulge like the back of the giant

Hermes dolphin salt sparkling dark come bearing::

Drowned

Open casket: a question of how they look: did look:—

salt lining in white rubber boots and pockets: wrapped in seine:

gunnel-bruised slightly on the forehead: still listening to what

the wind must have said: lashed by raiments

of rain: giving a last promise in return for everything still to come::

brine heaven: crabs who eat fishes fishes who eat crabs:

king fish: mako: hard-headed catfish: ravenous ibises curving above:

landburied without body: anchored: anchored:

yet still swimming in a hellish bright inlet:

seaweed in the beard: Odysseus too young for Troy:: so dreamed.

Eddy

Against wind's silk direction the tide is flowing,

turning on itself in the lee of salt marsh islands,

spiraling in large and little flowers that empetal

all below. The boat spins slowly and . . .

there'll come a change: yellowtail pulling on the line,

a closing of darkness: but, oh, in nature's matrix

for a few hours you lean neither away

nor toward . . . Whatever it is you refuse it.

Egret

Violent leaner: fallen earthward: unconscious

of body left by soul: I am moved by its marble pose

above winter water brown and frothed:

the tiny fish like stars on a cloudy night:

stars stars stars in water at its feet:

it makes its bleak adjustments and waits:

yellow bill held *en garde*: wind swirling

lashing: if only it could tell: how tides

must move through it: one fish never enough.

Low Tide

Leave leave me on a naked island

mud and encrustations of oysters glittering

where through some magic I may forget

the always passing of day and night

hands canceling hands on the clock face

of a lover parent friend:: already now

the gulf's gray waters tick against the grass

gulls laugh and cry above my stranded hull

will start to rock the channel river flow like Acheron::

But for a spell wasn't there quiet winter tide

lowest nothing beckoning—no passage at all?

Manatee

Shading to pink on the underparts: soft and liable

to be mistaken for Sirens: how sea sound comes

along the shore:: alone I found one shark-bitten deep

in the pelvic muscle floating near a shoal: water almost calm

light twinkling on oysters: fluting sweet shrill

fleur-de-lys: the western baths of early evening: clouds::

how we're saved from beauty beauty wanting

no other beauty but one:: with manatee in mind:—

gelid eye paddle-tail bloat—: my torn life myself surgeon-bitten::

my revocation:: in the mouth a pale root a word:

maculate flesh goldening as in a myth:: no more pretty songs.

Man So Bronzed

Forearms bulging lifting the giant cobia:

Xanthes river flowing from the west horizon:

wind subsiding, disintegrating, coming up::

maker of the gutted glistening fish

and maker of the evening: cold torrent in the eyes,

insolent ease in torso and hips: legendary

fish laid on the planks: burning river sinking

underneath the bay, darkness rocking, rippling—

you can hear it by the dock and feel the long day's motion

of the waves: a sort of dreaminess: the islanders

washing phosphorus from boats and gear:

sunset closing the marina. Haephestus murmuring:—

the quality of cobia: steel gone from sinew

smithy cool: then gone to supper.

Redfish

Loaves and fishes: coelacanth: Bishop's Jewfish:

the great silver fish that appeared to barter

life for three wishes: Tiburon: Eshark: Puffer:

Sharksucker: Hammerhead: Gag: in the riven waves

and rocking reverie of Florida sun they feed on grass

and each other: my trailing bait: smell of shrimp on fingers:

surface of water enameled: all all true—: the art and hell of it::

keep ammonia for catfish spines: loose the eye

or pluck it out: the lying on the side in water wiggle and flash

like resurrection—:: I'll tell you: north wind blew a recent morning

like acetylene: mud shone so and was freezing:

hands and feet burned with it: then the line swam upstream:

I came home marked with mud scales and fish slime:

mind in its parts admired the fight and iridescence

and remembered where to put the point of the knife:

blood swirled down the drain in the rinsing: I was happy::

What are living and dying if not the most natural

of ceremonies if practiced: not turned away from: not denied?

To Fishermen

No more savage art: filleting: a deft pressure along the backbone

from tail fan to the red gills: fighting mystery with a honed blade

through the small bones: salt and scales on face and hands:: the Greek God,

as well, found flesh unmysterious, but in anger and disappointment:—

sea gull cries, your music, are all about you: Apollonian but hungrier: nature is hungry::

the brave fish dies the birds swoop for the insides in no lovelier spirals.

Sea Hare

Gelatinous parching creature by the verge of the sea:

thick as a shoe: head dark green: sea a mixture of black

green blue: sky haunted by light rent with cries:

pelicans calling swimming in air folding wings

to dive into the sea: Bosch angels

changing shape as they're pursued from immaculate skies:

those few that accept the hideous and monstrous: fallen

a nightmare fauna—:: say the sea's to be questioned:

below the bounds of this estate though rainbowed cold

the rockheaded and cored of bone: chimera

our madness does not cease to reinvent and which we dare not

think alive crawl in a thick ooze: Yet even this one: torn

to the plain insides leaking dyes: exudes a gentle unrest of the soul::

Is it not good:: sea undulates: sharpening and smoothing

all the grooves history's graven in sand:: will you put hands

under the terrible flesh and heave it back to salt waters:

mirror of a lost estate: dawn-time of the world's first season.

Pelican

Rendings, grunts after so much quiet: look:

tide is advancing—billows, mullet leaping toward shore:

also pigfish pinfish herring sheepshead silverside grass and top

minnows prawns:: brown pelicans—Audubon drawn

chestnut cross-hatch iris blue rim reddened yellow tuft:

pistol-shot from wharves: beautiful evolutions

above the leaping shoal:: shot after shot::

made gumbo: salted: smoked: sensible to cold::

muting so profusely not a spot of green's left on the glossy mangrove::

esophagus storing fish: air pockets to cushion the blow:

black banners the drying wings after what is left

of watermire: wearing it: sitting in plainest light.

Clam

What the sea does and what the sea does

for Molluska: living in the gills of fish:: secreted a stony coat::

formed siphons anus stomach gills aorta foot::

the red tides come and go: bacterias salinities

boats storms:: compelling the imagination—Tarzan

in an African lagoon: giant lips around an ankle:

slitting the muscles and kicking free after breath's gone::

named cherrystone littleneck quahog *Moby's* Queequeg.

Now the water's sixty degrees and a fisherman

with Giacometti forehead seeds mesh bags

fish gone deep into channels and rivers shine cold::

not for its brilliant anatomy nor just for the money

does he work so in this America:— malls where thousands

of sweet meat pounds are bought—: not for the generations

drowning by drowning:: being alone sun and wind

in his face he said harvesting.

Orchid

In light's white rum in the light of the mind

bees come to the fertile stigmas

where with moderate degrees of force Darwin tested

Orchideae: the "wildest caprice"—

meaning cross-pollination: meaning their sensitivity

to pencil needles camel-hair brushes and his fingers::

Some wild orchids sicken by self-pollination::

others take on shapes so insects may alight thrashing calyx:

or resemble a pollinator's mate: smell luscious rotten::

so life spreads borne on a zephyr's back:: spreads

outside my window under the gold surface of water:

poured ointment of fishparts: dazing: whirling

through chambers of Byzantium:: mind's handiwork.

Boat

Miscalculation the day's first high

from the last moon gulf Hades dark:

at 3 a.m. shrimp boat run aground

and engine grinding who else awake:

window so silver it seemed not light

nor any natural element:

again and again a throttling up

spewing water propeller scoring

the mud until tide lifted the keel:

one might have thought it was the engine—

however it was the hull began

to move offshore the window blackened

I stood until all throbbing sound

was blotted out absorbed by the dark

interstellar caves near the horizon

turned to clouds in the stir of morning::

low tide revealed the diagonal

across a glassy flat mimic of

a comet tail following greater light—:

heaven and hell have no memory

nor message nor direction beyond

this human mark fast disappearing.

North Key

Blues browns sudden shallows tide possessing

our way to the farthest key: narrow outlet where someone

left white markers past which we weren't to go:

overturned hull biting salt and burning sun: temple

mounds in a time the Apostle Paul was writing

to Galacians: how can we not go on::

once we ran aground and were lifted

at daybreak: phoenix waters gray red: —

once I only raised the motor and poled

to deeper water:: charts often wrong: storm

shift: cuts narrowed:: still fathoming the tides

which seem not to change at all, not powerfully,

until all the basin shows and the sea's drenched

sound stops or starts anew: and sweet musk

of orchids is it? on a lunar breeze::

thus our revery for the farthest isle

continues and on the shoulders of wind terrors

glide we fly past rivers to enter the other world:

our faint footsteps on the marsh's mud rim.

And then, then what, what more?

Snake Key

Our sense of origin ourselves bedeviled:

Apollo Saturn: in the rose black garden Eve::

loving: killing:: labyrinthine the journey::

can't myth be left behind::

how it would be to start mid-kingdom::

standing by river water in marshes

never colored by another's eyes: saurian ripple:

flashing lances and silver spray of sunshine

through cat's claw palmetto: flung paths to the coast::

Muir describes two Negroes in firelight as devils:

they give him johnny cake: dire music

of the ibis he recalls: there are malarias:: wind

still fevers the tide: a small skiff lifts over the bar

to the outermost key: you can draw lime trees:

you can collect sea-worn shells:

you can count the snakes: you can:

but there's no way only back where you were::

Shore

Go out alone against the tidal river which does not care for you: —

what or who could care in the end more than you —:

fin and tail leave no trails and darkness simply comes and goes:

an orange moon mirrored in dead calm moves only along

not with you and all creation belongs to itself::

the thought will calm you and your return if you return: — say

if you hear thunder or pretty lights reach from shore

as far as you have gone —: you can ride the last fertile waters

inland:: who then will better know life like a rind

bobbing on the tide and who better know to speak of it?

Voyage

Dante-esque: staircase of birds descending: fish sparking

from the wet pyre: light that makes you feel day will never end::

I love and fear winding in these waters: deep corridors:

currents: shoals: irridescence boiling

suddenly: the back of something larger than my boat:

struck by light:: does the heart not darken: sins

sorrows winters:: but here coastal light—stellar

and enamel—isn't it the light—changes everything::

more than voyage:: with the great egret in slow glide

and manta ray—lion-colored: tail like Geryon—: by shell mounds

of the dead: wild marshes: wind rising: across

rugged gulf water: three rivers from cedar woods::

dark come evening and the crackle of stars!

II

Abstractions

*Absolute and eternal beauty does not exist . . . is only
an abstraction creamed from the general surface of different
beauties. The particular element in each manifestation comes
from the emotions . . .*

— Baudelaire

*Things we've let go of circle, and though we're rarely at
the center of these circles: they trace around us the
unbroken figure.*

— Rilke

Adultery

Had she repented? Given over? No. She let others talk and pretended
to listen. It must be borne—commandment, moral—but not digested.
Jonah was not digested. And wasn't the inside of the snare sweet as ambergris some days?
She would not be another washed up on a shore, whose saving must be explained.
She would be with all the rest; for the rest: salt, tides, crying gulls, crabs,
the ones who catch crabs, the ones who kill those ones. These were her self,
and she would not purge herself. If her integrity was in question,
no one spoke of it, yet in company she was restrained, like one who in a moment
may say something cooly funny or devastating; until then holding a shell to her ear,
        to hear all
the singer hears, with hand pressed lightly by the ear—harmonies and the thrilling
unadulteration of her own notes, darkened perhaps with losses, sorrows, but still luring.

Apology

Already the land is starting to forget gardens;
reminiscences no longer hold the heart completely
as someone held her a little roughly once in somber sweet groves,
and the touch she was utterly dissolute to, that caused collapse behind her knees,
sunslides in the lake, she feels a resistance toward, then apology,
as if a thorn catching her sweater has torn a small hole, —as if she shouldn't
have worn the sweater. What induces
then weakens the greater and lesser passions is what she'd like to know.
—Something like the green underneath red and yellow that is now wilting
has left her body; and she is someone who had loved
and is no longer availing and can neither take nor give away.

Art

Why, when she gave her memory a mother whose cruelty was godly,
and who was beautiful, and the North African boy of twenty
in the Paris of her youth, who tore down
his fresco at the end of every day because the cement hardened
before he could paint his red angels —*Je ne sais quand,* he'd say —,
and memory knew she loved them, did it refuse to say so? She imagined she saw its gorge fall,
as after swallowing, and her own mouth felt like cotton.
She wanted to write everything down. What could tell her she would have to forget herself,
her art, everything, and make herself stare at a lake where a dragonfly stared
at a tree, at nothing, then deposited its eggs in the still water and left,
as if it trusted or could go on without?

Balance

is how you carry it, how it is; for example, the turkeys that seemed ordinary—grazing
through the piled brush for butternuts, all head and feathers, then taking the shot because
they didn't see you standing on a stump,
one dying outright, the other baffled, half rising in the brown light and batted
to the ground—how ungainly large they made the afternoon, heaping up out of slopes,
trees, torn pieces of clouds
an excitement. When you stopped running, you took them from under your jacket,
where they had kept shifting and threatening to slip out,
still with a bit of warmth in them, and grasped one in each hand
by its horned feet like handles to steady yourself, leaning into the land's
steepness and accord, growing used to them, their difference.

Comfort

Because a sorrow was conquered, or a sin, can they relax?
No. Having felt hands crush and throw them down,
they see the ones in pieces everywhere and hear the eerie beat of their madness:
it trembles in the wings of hummingbirds, aloft as they eat, flying backwards.
So they persist without knowing how, and having been forbidden
presence, to push and cajole the ones on their knees—in balls, in their and others' beds,
in hell—to their feet so that they can find a way for themselves out into an airy place.
There they take down the hands flung before the face
and help to wash the inflamed portions of the others' hearts, so much like their own,
invisibly anointing whomever they can with oils, until and when the soft
pounding of their blood becomes comforting, like being held again in someone's arms.

Compatibility

Never after was life so filled with meeting,
with reuniting and drawing apart as then, when bed-hot, filled with surges,
the man and woman began to know each other.
It was like the makeshift walking of geese toward water, —a settling into themselves and,
with a fiercer and fiercer grip, a testing of the untried other. How safe they'd been before
they touched and he asked her one thing which she meant to resist but was unable to.
How beautiful to keep one's fabled eyes closed:—Was another's body not like some bright
obstruction? But they, as if they knew nothing, opened entirely, bending to two wills,
striking down vanities, feeling what lay deep inside—the darker compatibilities—
until love seemed causal, not just related.
Their sinuous tongues used the word, over and over, without speaking.

Conscience

The crow settles on a fir bough and disappears
(the way an usher waits by the threshold to the Old Dutch Masters' room
and watches. What does he think?). Not even the hunters and the dogs
are reminders that the crow exists, and it would seem that he would never come back,
reuniting with others in the winter sky and moving off,
until he does. A caw falls like a reprimand from his beak, and he emerges in his uniform black,
his wings trembling stiffly with their free ends. It is hard not to feel anger
at his assertion—how one feels life's unfairness, and little to help us in our hard choices.
What use the silence, semblance, and austere flying?
As the deep woods tower above, full of shapes, and the heavens threaten snow,
something is moving near as if it wanted to tear us from our molds:—as conscience is torn.

Crying Wolf

Not howling, but from within the deep wildness of all things—assailed on all sides
by the nightmare of nations, walking and flying specters, chimeras, nils,
which can't be outrun or waked, and which snows no longer bury—
came a sound as forlorn as when the heart devours the prophet. He lowered his head
at land's end after the wind took away the last of the sound and, in the silence,
the hair on the back of the neck of the world froze.

Custom

As if it had forgotten everything—hatred, vindictiveness, the meaning of pain—
the bull took the ribboned sticks in his back without response, turning away,
so that when the picador entered the ring, the crowd was making fun
of the country's breeders. If there was an ounce of dignity or strength in the animal,
the picador would have to find it with his pole, and he came on slowly
to probe the back and shoulders:— cruelly, like a king with a scepter.
The bull barely moved until the picador gambled all and sailed his beautiful hat
   into the air above
the lowered head. With that the bull's will broke and he rushed again and again
like a child, a superbly angry prince, at the horse's side. When it was over, the bull
and its retinue gone inside to the abbatoir, the picador reentered the ring.
The assembly roared—by his actions they knew they knew better who they were.

Ecstasy

Her ecstasy rises like a rider on a leaping horse
and she knows to push through it calmly and completely, without rushing
or closing her eyes. The ground falls away, the sky, precipitate,
whirls about her shoulders, and she feels both saturated with motion and still.
If she thought (there is barely time), could it be of love's reciprocal
demands to give and be given?—as if an Angel appeared in the heart
and spoke: As your body rocks so shall his. So it seems,
because her hands, which were resting, begin
dreamily to stroke his neck and sides.
When she leans forward to whisper—a fondness and encouragement—
she is within herself again, exhilarated, and strangely proud.

Envy

Look: the cat lifts its head, switching its tail, and to the other cat says
in a voice almost too low to hear, something angry, interrupting their shared meal.
Hissing, they both stand absolutely
still—quivering, full of mistrust—equally, it seems, over the bowl with its morsels
of flesh, though one must start to feel the other's resolve greater than her own;
or the other fetches from within a hardness like a beautiful blade
from a locked cabinet; because the first breaks away and walks to the other side
of the room. While the other's eating recommences, she springs onto the pampered chair
and sits looking out the window at the birds flitting by, if cat eyes don't blur
at that distance, then suddenly turns her head down to her chest
in a burst of envy to lick and lick her own fur.

Fate

Imagine: in the twilight of a river, trout rising to the hairs and netted wings
of water walkers, and yourself casting a baited line
toward shadows. There is no talking, and the mind learns
to drift, to take in the slightest signs, as if there's already begun
under the surface what will come to pass; it lures you along.
Reed, ripple, raccoon-scratches on the mud bank
lend their wisdom and their indifference to the moments before the pole bends double
or you give up, walk to the lighted house, and join the others at a table
to talk of life, love, logic and the senses, memory, promise, betrayal, character
and fate—the driving notion
that around the river bend a magnificent fish waits, prickling the black water.

Fury

And the whole night she had told herself to be pleasant
as she lay by the sleeping man, and she'd gladly have listened to herself,
but as the enormous dawn sneaked into their darkness
and seized them in its paws, she found herself with the old fury,
past her carefullest politeness. She saw she'd need millennia to find a way
to comprehend the reason for the difference between their early ideals—
a garden where plums and peaches grew well and tasted wild
and they were unembarrassed by genitals—and what had become of them.
This apple-pose. It was no good blaming God or Adam, she knew,
    but she couldn't help herself.
Why hadn't the one spoken forthrightly and had the other caved in?
Then, hardly allowing him to fully awaken, she spoke her first sarcasm. Then another.

Harm

She had only begun to get used to her body's exposures
to pain, like the insinuations behind questions: winter
asking the tree, where's your strength?—a priest asking a soul, where's your marrow?
Aversions, truth, invective,
it wasn't her answers which mattered, only her lying on a bed
being administered shocks until the world grew tired
of experimenting with another bit of clay and the inward liberties. So it seemed.
And when the intern came into the room, asking how she was
and snouting through her chest with drainage tubes, as strong a desire
as she'd ever had rose up in her. She must have gestured or he already knew because
as if in expectation, he smiled at her and stepped backward, out of harm's way.

Her Beauty

By now her beauty no longer catches glances like small animals in a gentle snare,
autumn having thinned the light and frozen its blossoms in the field.
Even her looks of imprecation and her frowns seem weak,
and she says fond, foolish things about herself,
about once having been greatly admired, envied, fated—
a Psyche to Venus—and how she loved her husband who gave her pleasure
and was faceless. Better than pretending
indifference—like the heaping snow;
better to say what she by another once had known,
only so secret and withdrawn the way it is in mornings,
in weather, an animal's fur bristling, a mole skin.

Homo sapiens

In this lonely, varying light of dawn with the residue of desire
like mist departing, I am walking. Was it in your eyes,
where my elongated face shone, I saw for the first time —
as if all the transparent fire in these trees had become palpable —
a hunger that was not wholly animal?
The need to tremble like dogwood, feeling the rain touch down.
My strange blood rises, and I may see you, fair leaves slipping over you, half-hidden
in the morning. With the beasts beside a pond,
I conjure the inward sun to leap into my brain. What remains?
Wild, beautiful petals all around.
A beast's face. And something, something else.

Horror

When horror, that with pretty masks
no longer stood to one side as he walked from his house to the garden,
extolling neither the magic of the atmosphere nor medals he earned for painting,
but undefinable, still deferred
(as if somewhere a prophet had put down his hood and bellowed),
grew colossal, Goya put fourteen black versions on his interior walls,
the most audacious a dog whose trespasses have sunk him in an abstract grave.
That he cannot go to the Master toward whom he is looking is in the slight blue stain
in the dog's eyes; that Goya wanted the whole room to see how terribly the dog wanted
to go is in the tipped yellow absence above his head. This is how it was and how it is:
caught, wholly tempted, without a clue. How little has art driven off.

Imagination

Imagine that there are several paths. But none takes her
away. Whether she goes past the laid-up stones of the dam and a pent-up pond,
or into some foreign silent meadow with raspberry canes, she returns to the same
shaded entrance, as if she could never err; her mind won't let her.
Numbed and insane, she feels like someone's trapped creature:
a weatherbeaten sylph holding onto a gate.
Why doesn't she just go, avoiding turns to the left and right,
until *everything* behind her is unfamiliar, unrelated; and she can be utterly new?
You may ask, but what do you know with your maps, books, and clocks? Stuck
as you are, will you yank off the silent dial face and, taking no counsel,
walk unfettered into the wild north fields?

Joy

Ah, that Noah's joy lasted only for a time presses itself on the heart and mind.
When they called him foolish, he went on building.
But then among the drowned like soaking marionettes the ark bobbed, so that even
his closest friend meant *nothing* to the Father:—How could he hold to his beliefs?
Like the caged beasts roaring, and as the wind beat itself on the water and the hull,
wouldn't he have liked to ease himself with yelling? Suddenly it comes to you:
he did yell. The trust he'd flung out with such abandon was absorbed by the gray pall.
And you harden yourself against the appearance of the landbird
—as if sunning his anguish and walking in washed and earth-spiced air
could rid the nostrils of the stench of the past forty days—,
a consummation that makes the sweat grow cold.

Laws

She knows of doom only what all women know,
deciding not to speak of it, since speech pretends
its course can be made to bend:—someone fleeing hot and sweating
and the victors close behind, then two roads all at once in a wood. Which one leads
farther away? Under cover of silence
she goes along as if perhaps nothing would happen to her,
seeming to be swayed by breezes—dazed, her friends say in their concern,
after, when they've thought of it, having called or dropped by.
Once, though, late in her illness, in the heat of a morning walk,
she raises her wig and shows us this surge of white back from the forehead. The tablets
Moses carried, with his guesses, in the end could not have been more blinding or more lawful.

Lies

Isn't there a race of people made of glass, who when spilling
too much of themselves on someone's sofa, in someone's house, act shattered?
They have come to the party as if in someone else's place,
perjuring with too-little-allowed and agreeable nods themselves:
When they laugh with the general laughter, it's a queer, ceramic chiming.
Who invited them? It's as if, wanting to fit in, they would give promise after promise,
limitless and indistinct, and as if they were their own diaries no one must read
except for a few paragraphs that contain modest wording for what is not meaningless
nor all lies. On timid feet they carry themselves through the knots of men and women—;
every voice's tone is as if to be avoided, as if cold every other person's bearing—;
until one of their great sorrows falls from their lips. And then apology.

Mind

As he went on—no one else in the yard, late, well past dinner—stacking cordwood,
it was as if his body, supple and allayed
by sweat, were surrendering to something larger than itself, unpossessed
by moonlight, so that when from the shadows, head-
first, exhausted, August fell, he sensed it; it was neither the wind,
nor the dark that so increased in all things they almost perished,
but more like a theater curtain drawn back—: There stepped
lives not completely lived
yet inflamed, and a wooden staircase. Out of death and promises he'd made,
his mind, in rhythm with the lateness of the world,
that turning, saw absence and its presentiments step down, as if free.

Music

You are right. At death I might well desire both day and rest,
some calm place where light is stabilized on an arbor,
a table, green glasses, and damask. The taste is of earth and sunlight,
tomatoes with folds at the blossom end and a large rough navel
with a bit of stem still attached, oil with basil
and lots of garlic, causing thirst for wine. And the music
to be played at the funeral must be the sound of the rosined bow
working against the wind, not old keys that are only echoes, but strange
gold in the beetle's click, a jay, a three color bird, a brown thrush,
their asides and intimations like the napkin songs
of great composers, written before the last bread and wine are gone.

Nothing

She turned away. And her child slid toward
the ice edge of the precipice, gravity and momentum wrestling on his shoulders.
She could not bear to see the outcome and was starting to pretend he did not exist,
if his existence would come to an end. See: there is a snowy peak and clouds
spilling so softly they create a whirlpool of silence. She lets herself be in it.
She no longer hears anything. Not the wind. Not the scraping shoes. Not him.
How she used to fret, to brush the hair back from his eyes
so everyone could see his beauty and she could see the least shadow
of sorrow or illness. But there is nothing left to do for him.
Since the forces like acrobats keep somersaulting and playing
with him, she will not hearken or give them the pleasure of her scream.

Obsession

Never was life more nervous, sweeter, denser than nutmeat
and honey than when she was obsessed with who she was.
It was like passing between two mouths a morsel, thinking of swallowing later, if at all:
—Narcissus at daybreak rinsing his forehead and watching the beautiful tears.
If he stayed an eternity on his knees, why couldn't she?
But something interfered, asking her to weigh once more from the beginning
her gravity against her alibis:—the responsibilities—
till she put back the dividing walls inside her mind.
From time to time at night or when she walks alone in a summer field the delicious sense
still returns to her, God knows from where, and she believes she is different,
as if from a far off world.

The Past

Was it in stepping into dusk? Did a glance release this turbulence
where Martin's fields thicken with thorn apple and a migratory bird
makes a sound?
Not even the quick flowering of April winds alters it, what a man in a straw hat
bending down
above the scythe's reach found, only now so saturated with rust and greatly indrawn,
the way it is in the past.
Yet the blade seems to will itself to hold an edge, expressing the kind of time
which plays around the roots of the grasses, and still knows, still passes,
still causes shadows
to seem to fit themselves around the ankles, refusing separation.

Pure

He saw that the white-tailed deer he shot was his son;
it filled his eyes, his chest, his head, and horribly it bent on him.
The rest of the hunting party found him hunkered down in the grass,
spattered like a butcher, holding the body as it kept growing colder in his arms.
They grasped his elbows, urging him to stand, but he couldn't. He screamed then
for Mary and Jesus, who came and were present. Unable to bear
his babbling , and that he might no longer have to be reproached, the men went to get help.
He only had left to him his pure hunter's sense, still clean under his skin,
and a gun, the example of wounds, a shell's ease in the chamber, as he loaded,
and the speed of the night chill, while his mind like a saint's tried to bear
that which God took from His own mind when he could not, not for another moment . . .

Recompense

That time, long practiced in pinning the alligator's jaw between his chin and chest,
the wrestler swam wearily, with long, blind hands and arms,
toward the brown eyeknobs, ignoring the crush and pester of the crowd
above the gator hole. And when the reptile bit,
he felt himself torn open, left exposed, accused—: fiercely,
that somehow a new existence could be formed out of the old. He remembers he rotated
with the alligator, attending to its muscularity,
pulling it down to the river bottom where its heart gave out and it drowned.
He tore the white belly skin for a belt. He took the stomach stones
as recompense for his disfigurement. — All the while saving the crowd's glances,
which were tinged with respect, though some wept and some looked at the darkening bayou.

Scorn

She thought of no wilder delicacy than the starling eggs she fed him for breakfast,
and if he sat and ate like a farmhand and she hated him sometimes,
she knew it didn't matter: that whatever in the din of argument
was harshly spoken, something else was done, soothed and patted away.
When they were young the towering fierceness
of their differences had frightened her even as she longed for physical release.
Out of their mouths such curses; their hands huge, pointing, stabbing the air.
How had they not been wounded? And wounded they'd convalesced in the same rooms
and bed. When at last they knew everything without confiding—fears, stinks,
boiling hearts—they gave up themselves a little so that they might both love and scorn
each other, and they ate from each other's hands.

Secrecy

It lay and dried in the sun, puffing, then losing its coherence,
and there was a sudden sickliness
in the air when the wind lifted and blew across to her, as if in ambush: cotton
and sweet chloroform. She ducked down and away, holding her breath, and went on
until she could sense no longer what ran from the raft of skin.
It was as if someone had risen up, unwashed, bearded, from a copse,
and tried to come too near—with a gesture of supplication, knowing
that she was half-willing, tempted by strangeness (a bouquet
of lilacs in a beggar's hands)—and almost succeeded. But it grew
too intense, menacing. She shied. It was scarcely explainable
and could not be kept a secret. A branch lightened into place.
Everywhere things decayed.

Self

They left her alone; it was what she wanted.

The bay waters had not been so secret for a long while, their great labor quiet.

She rowed over the calm of the ebb to an island of birds—heron, cormorant, egret waiting
in the tall mangroves, placid and self-contained, as if she alone were meant to see them
and find some meaning there. She back-watered through the down-strewn shallows
until one by one, then faster, all the birds rose, clucking, in some tribal crescendo.

    Immense cloud

heads stood close above, like the whitened manes of blind and venerable gods,
gods, who remembering the fresh lands—now so remote—listened hard for the least shout
of anger or amazement. For a moment she felt she had pleased them,

though that hadn't been her intention, and no one else knew. But it remained in her:

what soared: the fierce rush: birds crying fear: and herself the cause.

Sex

If, as with a flock of sexless sheep, gently and without craving
they walk beside each other for days, not pressing, —only let either's depth stir
and the other wants to soothe and understand. With fingers, elbows, breastbones.
One has had one's anger, one's faction, one's guarded place
no one can get into, least of all one so close;
yet who would believe the almost lethal force one wants to strike with sometimes,
as beasts hurt each other, biting, clamping onto the wounded neck.
What is more potent and familiar? Wasn't she the one in whom
many times the other lost himself? Can he be in any other person more?
If Venus can be of little further assistance to this pair,
when she surges through the one, the other is dragged there—was, and will not go away.

Sexual Jealousy

Think of the queen mole who is unequivocal,
exuding a scent to keep the other females neuter
and bringing forth the colony's only babies, hairless and pink in the dark
of her tunneled chamber. She may chew a pale something, a root,
find it tasteless, drop it for the dreary others to take away, then demand
more; she must suckle the young. Of course
they all hate her and are jealous of the attention given her
by her six bedmates. In their mutual dream she is dead and her urine
no longer arrests their maturing. As irises infallibly unfold,
one of their own will feel her sex grow quickest and greatest. As they dig
together, their snouts full of soil, they hope this and are ruthless in their waiting.

Soul

They took off their clothes a thousand nights
and felt the plaster of the moon sift over them, and the ground roll
them in its dream. Little did they know the light and clay and their own sweat
became a skin they couldn't wash away. Each night bonded to the next,
and they grew stiffer. They noticed this in sunlight—there were calluses,
round tough moons on their extremities,
shadows under their eyes, and sometimes a faint sour smell they hadn't had as children.
This worried them, but at night the animal in their bodies overcame their reluctance
to be naked with each other, and the mineral moon did its work.
At last when they woke and were dead, statues on their backs in the park,
they opened their mouths and crawled out, pitifully soft and small, not yet souls.

Thrill

To say fabricated things, where freedom is forced on young girls,
and give it your own sensual twist, pretending in their bodies'
natural curves lies a willingness like animals to lick and rub each other
in the soft afternoon light. To thrill yourself with the imagined scent
of bodies redolent with oil and mango-colored.
And if a child's face releases a shadow,
no longer able to quiet herself with herself (*what*, for you, is wrong?),
to force her on to an ever deeper bliss—a nude queen lying on a green carpet,
a servant picking yellow fruit, and two old men near a large tree
discussing The Tree of Knowledge, your favorite scene.

Waking

It was dusk, the light hesitating and a murmur in the wind, when the deer, exhausted,
turned to look at me, an arrow in its side. Though I pity dreamers,
taking a thread and weaving it upon the loom of Self—
the secret, gaudy, wonderful new cloth—, I will tell the end of the story.
His shoulder was torn, the joint held by one sinew, which I severed with the arrow blade,
so when he ran there were no impediments. The black dogs that followed were swifter,
their barking ancient and despicable.
As he fell, his chest turned to breastplate, his one powerful arm covered with pagan signs.
Nearly stupid in my waiting for what would happen next, each breath propelling me and
him toward dust, I woke, the sheets soaked, heart fluttering—: When death
comes into the sleeping room as through a tiny hole, like a rent in the Covenant, it hurts.

Wilderness

Thought is a wilderness like Bartram's—razed, cemented over, marked by rows
of parked cars and citizenry stones of those less and less well remembered.
It is Muir's *glorious forest* and turpentine factories, and Audubon's pistol shots.
For thought, like Audubon's, contains birds of every description, the pretty one on my sill
with painted crest and impossibly red bill and feasting vultures.

                                        The commotion
in so much stillness lured me nearer in my kayak and I waved my paddle high
when the vultures circled back for more of the carcass, scattered and rotten.
Thought possesses and is possessed by bits of history. And Arcturus, and the house lights
in cities, when there is no other light. And the human
voice, your laughter in the null moment,
at null o'clock before one last good night.

III

Apiary Poems

. . . honey . . . is engendered from the air, mostly at the rising of the constellations . . . and then just before day-break. Hence it is, that at early dawn the leaves of the trees are found covered with a kind of honey-like dew, and those who go into the open air at an early hour in the morning find their clothes covered, and their hair matted, with a sort of unctuous liquid. Whether it is . . . the sweat of the heavens, or whether a saliva emanating from the stars, or a juice exuding from the air while purifying itself . . . falling from so vast a height, attracting corruption in its passage, and tainted by the exhalations of the earth . . . deteriorated besides by the juices of flowers, and then steeped within the hives and subjected to such repeated changes — still . . . it affords us by its flavour a most exquisite pleasure, the result, no doubt, of its aethereal nature and origin.

— Pliny the Elder

1

(For the ones
who line the corridors and sit
silent in wheelchairs
before the television with the volume off,
whose cares
are small and gray and infinite,
time as ever to be faced . . .
Methusalas the nurses wash
and dress without haste—
none needed . . .
this one has drunk from the poppy-cup
and drowses in her world of dream . . .
Heliotrope,
carnations, wakeful violets, and lilies in vases—
masses of flowers—wrap
the urine-and-antiseptic air in lace . . .
Please wake up; it is morning;
robins whistle; the bees dance.
Isn't this other one listening
from her shell of silence,
and shouldn't she smile at the green return
and dappled light through windows.
As earth orbits the corridor
clocks are wound . . .
The last hour is a song or wound . . .
Except in this corridor—mother's—
where finity's brainless wind
blows ash, and ash again
blows through their cells:
So much silence, so little to say in the end.)

2

Pearly flying hair,
shirt lit with spring flora
and zephyrs, she is a wedding
unto herself. We're leaving
the hall where George jazzes
a piano for the only one dancing.
The others were exhausted
before they arrived,
but she announces the sweetness
of earth and of sky—
she may as well be intoxicated. We like
to say so. It's the purpose
of a wedding.
She is dancing. We won't say
she's dying. George came to her room
to get her, smiled toward us,
we handed her over,
in the hall, and then we went
out the front door
whose code
few there remember.

3

Abandoned bee boxes piled on each other at meadow end . . .
Like clothing taken off,
the bees who had alighted on hat,
gloves, shirt, have flown off somewhere.
Is it so terrible to outlive the mind?
Forget this, forget that—keys, glasses,
what it was you just said, what you meant to say.
Pseudonyms. Silences:
oddball or golden and grave, a dance of signs,
sorrows passing by like shadows,
time running by like a small girl running by like a madwoman.

4

(Tyrannus tyrannus)

That bird towering: late summer
garden: who senses the burring wings
deep inside roses and like the angel
before all nectar's sipped
before gold scatters in bright air
descends from its high height
to lift away the bee . . .
not a honey eater: though looking so:
bee after bee disappearing
into incandescence.
Only the metaphysic flower
feels the approach: and emptying.

(Ursinus)

Gold helm scent of honey and the drowsing bear:
golden: begotten of honey: bee larvae
chokeberry sweet clover carrion:
leaving the den in the undergrowth
for sweet-thaw sun-thaw above:
shut out from all the world within.
The valleys and hills feel its feet
shambling when the sun is low:
slow mouth. Didn't mother say she felt
its presence a long time?
Thought small as atoms
and aromatic as honey ales:
body manacled—body preserving
small sweetnesses?
Until the bear groaned and stretched:
entered there and deeply ate?

5

I remember the psychiatrist's exam—
Draw a clock.
Hers was a stone sun dial,
numbers rubbed away.
Try again, and she quartered the day,
but there were no hands
to lift and drop sunlight
and moon's cold clay.
How exposed she was—
dark, cruel
moment when she found out—
mind a papery hive sliced
open, herself furious.

6

Then it was autumn.
Each morning she would rise and dress
and walk out the back door where orange rounds
hung from boughs—breasts, big acorns, eggs, jewelry bags?
She waited, she told me, for the right word
to come back to her. Maybe she stood on the patio a few minutes
or hours. The closing click of the door behind her
made her look back, and she stepped inside.
I don't think I believed her then. The weeks passed,
the months, then her forgetfulness blended with angers,
as if red wild bees were knocked from large red blossoms
by witches. When she began her wandering
along cracking pavement, by blank billboards, toward lights
that in the distance must have seemed mythic (or she slept,
intent on making time go away, like a vagrant),
then I felt hushing in her before, by dark severance,
flesh no longer could feed the sweetest mind.
Honeycomb, goddess, death, fate, and the human heart,
they lived in her until too many of her words
flew like birds of the muses away, so few at first
that their disappearance didn't much matter.

7

Two anthills and a late summer hive
gone to fragments.
The dirt is acrid, the wax honeyed —
so mind makes laws, dividing seasons,
scents, light and light's reflections.
I have no mother. Yes, you have a mother,
a voice said. But that is not right. Her difference —
a broken hive . . . a black bear in the bluebells
clawing the stinging air . . . something torn from her.
Still, the land soothes me — *No one may come* — :
low sun, dusk, and charred trees,
seeming first to glow as they darken, really are only darkening,
as if autumn burned.
And if I want it otherwise, O Self,
there's beauty in small lies.
I say bees lick nectar after dark
and bring it to the bough of the honey tree.
Royal jelly keeps the larvae from falling
from the cells. *Broodcomb, honeycomb, bee bread —*
this is a harmless thought. Yes, once I had a mother.
I said to her, there is no twenty
on the clock, don't worry. I said
I will tell you the time. She said how little it takes
to finish . . . *What?*
Stupid, Orphean things swirl:
Apricot flowers . . . bees circling
as many times as the distance to the nectar. . .
throbbing wings . . . *buzzing* . . .
then to pluck the mind from darkness
singing. Mother hears
ambient grief and, more and more,

her earlier German tongue—rhyming, Schiller lines.
Where were you? I'll ask. *Wer bist du,* she'll say,
winter in voices, drifting,
snow drift, freezing, the bees dropping
to the hardpan inner darkness . . . O Mother . . .

8

As if by amber or in Lethe's stream
she has been caught, yet still I find it strange
I cannot reach her, who says I look like her.
Where is her mind? A glimmer sometimes forms
as dawn forms on the horizon, but she sorrows
until it's dark again and she no longer knows
that thing from this. The organic
earth and the universe seem themselves to pulse
with Time and leave behind their proofs:
pictured constellations and ancient insects
whose molecules for brain motion
exist in us. We go on living,
this year's renewing sap still untasted
above the heaped decay of last fall
when she first lost her way.

9

The honeycomb is made from flowers
and the materials for wax bees gather
from the resinous gum of trees,
while honey is distilled from dew.

At the rising of the constellations
or when a rainbow is in the sky,
the dew is deposited in the comb.
Dew from sweet-tasted flowers.

This, mother, is my song for you
pretending to sleep with open eyes.
As odor and dance lead bees to nectar,
though you're far away I will come to you.

10

You suddenly wearied. You had to sit
under the sun's force, chilled and sweating,
that hot afternoon in Key West. I think it was 1997.

Your eyes grew very bright. Like two zig-zag butterflies,
time and your sense of it spiraled out
over the water. (I'm not sure of the date.)

A ship rumbled in the harbor,
the burning sky was intent on the water.
I'll try to remember the exact date.

You couldn't follow their course
past a certain point, but this was the onset
of your forgetfulness. I told you—Key West in 1997.

What date (not to all, but to you and to me
the year is of importance)? Remember. It was
a hot afternoon in Key West. 1997.

A little problem with space and time, we used to say,
when the diagnosis sounded too harsh.
What year was it, you ask? 1997.

It couldn't have been hotter.
Yes, Key West. No, not honeybees—two butterflies.
You know the year.
1997.

11

Amid a menagerie she sleeps as in a lair—
lion, bear, and wolf bedded in rich darkness,
the air sweet with opiates—and when she wakes
refreshed, small lights in her clear animal eyes,
it's easy to imagine that the animals have spoken
in a dream of the allegorical life:
Out of the wounded side honey issues.
In light, dementia exposes the sweet lie.
She gazes but rarely speaks—tree names, German
flowers haltingly knot on the string
she once could string without thought.
The question of her being, of whether she was,
insisted on being asked. If once
the beauty in photos
all knew, how could she be
this other—fervorless and gaunt—or wasn't
the mirror cracked? And with the stinging truth
came her need for more and more sleep
in flowered bedclothes, with the animals
with fixed eyes who seemed to have been
waiting for her still sexual scent and weight
to dream them again all into life.

12

Odor plume, mellifluous humming, thick syrup
made from nectar, calyx: cave of bees—
wild eden come to this: a room next to a similar room
where women are cared for. *Where are the men?*
my mother asks in a tone suggesting God's interference.
There was one who gardened, his head bent
over a bed of roses; between her and him only a window
patched with glass emblems of stars. She tapped,
he smiled. Then he was sent away, but left for her
a drawing of a horse, pawing with front hooves
the bottom of the yellow page of paper
torn from a notebook; otherwise motionless
as if in amber. Her daughter-in-law taped it to the wall.
She broods on darkness as it seals her room,
then broods on dawn, as if they were the same—
time before the archangel came to punish
when Eve and Adam swayed on Eden's gate
and couldn't yet leave.

13

It was August, it was August
and she was dancing, no, we three were dancing.
Her paranoia wasn't yet Thracian.
I thought of the greenhouse in Vienna,

my grandmother, her mother, dancing
while her partner's wife sat stone-lipped
among roses in the Viennese greenhouse.

I was young, what do the young know
of forgivable sin? I was stone-lipped.
My husband was singing, while dancing,

his sin his innocence—how old must one be to know
that sexual beauty is dangerous at any age?
My husband sang *Embraceable You* and danced,

mother dipped toward him, and he turned
to her. She'd want to tear him to pieces,
but she didn't know that

until in the end he spurned her—
her mind jangled like bees in a sac.
But she didn't know that.
It was August, it was only August.

14

If her falling to quiet
after harsh years reversed, where
would it start if not before irony,
hurt, want, sex?
Time's soft machine goes past
this spring, and last, past
Lascaux and the first magnifications
on stone, before the first look in a pool,
the first I am, and back
before tongues licked
nectar, wings fanning honey, and body
carrying sexual powders
through conifer forests
to begin the abominable diversification
of flowers, back to rain,
to the first drop crashing.

15

To live without memory is to have each hour
as a pane of air for canvas and the view from a window
to paint: amber-honey cold mornings:
humbled by evening: variation and variation
of ambiguous figments—ziggurat beehive
auroras—flicker and go out. All history
may as well be in these brushstrokes:
the hand has not rested nor the paint dried.

16

As small lamps drift with river tide
and against the wind, her revery keeps wavering,
her gaze inward. Beyond is the dark, chopped bay,
beyond no lights at all. Couldn't she step
ashore to a place with its own name
and return, knowing the difference
between there and here? She has told me
of the sea in legendary depth and darkness,
the moon's huge black bulk, apparitional
salt lilies in the blind valleys of the ocean's floor
brain blots—no stars at all, no, no
spindrift light, no nearness
that in sudden whirlpool
doesn't sink and cease to remember.

17

Beauty and dust, beauty and dust—
but to simplify we say dementia
(time sensing, recognizing, recollecting
soon ceasing), unable to imagine the fields along Lethe
dim lit but with their few flowers: corolla
and grains of pollen for the ancient bees.
"A little problem with space
and time," she and I first kidded,
is becoming no place and perilous travel,
days harsher than mineral. Lethe
is someplace. Water laps against
a wooden boat. In time of frankness, lie.
Tell her she will come soon with you home.

18

All things are taken from us
and in a little while our cares
are numb. Lotus pollen wafts
through the valleys and shadows.

Our bodies outlast us, sleep-
wandering in the spiced mist,
even as we sit. We sip the cup
if it is offered. Is it milk?

To taste would be
a simple perfection of thought—
the brain's wild bee that grows
honey seeking bee rose.

Swollen with dust and rain
and rumor, our eyes grow inward.
It is restful knowing nothing
more, knowing no one any more.

19

The mind is no tunnel deepening
to a pent element, perhaps an underground lake
of undrinkable waters,
bottom silted over
with names of objects and the people
she has known all her life. She can recite
Die Lorelei and recognizes the Dalai Lama
but not you. Sure, you want to know how
she can talk politics and laugh
but not ladle up a family memory.
It helps to read a book,
change her prescription,
see in her clouded eyes
breezes of light,
think of the myth of the mantis,
who in its exhaustion was laid
on a floating flower. In its thigh
a seed was left, the bee flew on,
all people came to life,
and nothing yet themselves
drank minutes shut in the water.
"Why am I here?" they asked,
and answered then, "To see what comes,
beginning first faintly to look like
something, some parts missing,
fish fins, for instance. We *almost* see it:
turning into gilly, or red butterfly
in water, on black sand. Crisp gills,
insect petals, rose-red, and the even darker,
accurate rose of blood. Then words
rooted at the bottom of the lake,
or agitating the heart."

Said so (their heads dripping with water),
it will be hard to turn away.
But remember the woman
in her dementia who is half dead.
The myth is too pretty.

2 0

"Generous I may have been, amnesiac
I became. Autumn fattened and thinned;
I stared at the clock's senseless hands.
I let the girl in the market make change.
I looked at my lists of medicines
and the bottles on the shelf, but they
seemed separate. In the bathroom mirror
my face was suddenly antediluvian *who*
was I? I'd be thinking and at the first touch
of attention, I'd forget. I cut my own hair.
I saw my mother wrapped in a mantilla
in her coffin. Why did I find my skin's
imperfections so interesting and pick off
moles? If I went to the end of the street,
would I be at the center of myself?
Insects watched me. They got in my hair.
I'd be at the opera house in Vienna.
The planes strafed the Strassenbahn.
My hands fluttered then like butterflies.
For a little while I knew—there was a door,
a split in the wall, and I was two persons,
old and young, wise and clean, sturdy and
bent, generous and dead. They were
neck on neck like winter and spring
but could do nothing for each other.
I'm leaving, I know, each said,
a flooding darkness in their eyes,
a drawing down of blinds. Afterwards
my feelings were the eyes of moths.
They . . . What is the word between eyes

and too little light? I knew. I think so.
Meanings fissured. Words hollowed.
It was like the thing with bees—
I swatted in front of my face
and hated them. Then there were none."

Light clear in a window, morning
finding white flowers, herself climbing
in the Alps alone to the meadow
of edelweiss and descending
at dusk — rock and field slurring . . .
In her corner room she sleeps and grieves,
bedclothes like dirty plumage.
Light and lamp now drug her.
She was the child Sorrow
in *Madama Butterfly.*   Stattsoper
Haus.   Bombs, strafing,
gut of some war? Where are stones
that were her city?
Who kissed her?
I want to hear those stories,
but she may as well be lyre
and head on a black river, singing
to no one.
A hundred answers within her burn.
When I (*You look like me who are you?*) tell her
the words Marlene Dietrich,
the Marlene she loves, sings,
the melody won't coax the hours.
Her mind's a bedraggled swan on a black river.

2 2

Why are we here, who owns this house
she asks: The dark place she thinks is
an ocean at 3 a.m.: no stars or moon:
She's swimming alone.
Chocolate dribbles to her chin:
We feed her chocolate because
she likes chocolate and she
forgets *Who owns this house   Why* . . .
We walk in her garden:
We hold on to her elbows: Here's the fruit
honey fungus in the hive
where we all may end our days—
anonymous, named . . . Ought not
to make elegies out of our fear
but we do. Yesterdays wilt:
the smoke for calming
bees drifts to our heads::
Why are we here in this state:
the landscape flowing away: tides
disturbing the shore?
Whoever comes after can gather
those bumping on the disturbed shore.

2 3

The humble sense of being alive
under the towering sun
fills the nectary and ripens apricots
down to the last one,
if Mnemosyne wakens from apathy
each moment. It is the soft burly sound
of a bee tumbled in fritillary,
is it not?
But if memory, as if to illustrate
the mind was not yours to have,
the mind was not given,
fails us, leaving us in our underpants
in the garden, should we not
hate the garden,
or the woman whose garden
it is? And sunlight. Thunder.
Rain. Hardened in heart against
what earth compels and seizes,
god-damning, god-damned rain.

2 4

Pretty to think of the mind at its end
as a metaphysician beekeeping
after the leaves have fallen at autumn's end:

Never sweeter, closer, those hours
before the pears fell. Were not the cells and stars
fruit-smelling? Where are those hours?

In the ashes of old pains and joys, in the burning
and nectar, the interstellar black garden,
the cold solstice, space inside a space once burning.

The wintriest gray shape, beauty
smoked out—no longer full of rapture, sweet lies,
(See, the beekeeper's terrible blank eyes are trying

to make whoever looks see that he no longer knows
what to think, do, feel, or even what day it is, and he succeeds.)—
but a blunt empty box.

I see the unmarked snow,
the yawning tree, shriveled bees
on the bottom pan, and I see dead beauty.

She wears geegaws from relatives
who smile when she tells of thieves
coming with any change of light,
when she drowses late or leaves her room early.
She has hidden and can't find her amethyst
and rain sapphire.
There was the gold necklace
she wore as naturally as a sun bear's golden bib,
the clasp so strong the thief in the subway
a world ago couldn't break it,
dragging her along the platform
as if along the dark ramparts
of a besieged city.
Where, now, has that been put?
Old, did Helen wear diadems?
Did she know glass from diamonds?
Her daughter-in-law admires the box ribbon
wound around her wrist. She smiles
and winds her bracelet once more
with little apprehension
of small evils and lies.
I'll give it to you, she says. Later on.

2 6

She saw that the tortured dream wrestled to the floor
was a gray-haired woman. She saw
the walls and connecting corridors of Legacy Heights
as prison, and when the nurses phoned her son,
he took away her telephone as punishment
for hallucination. She knew this for a few days,
then forgot. *Were her phantasies*
drug-induced? I asked the staff. They looked
at each other. I asked my brother. He said,
Why isn't she able to rejoice with joyous dreams?
Why is she so negative? Irremediable, the being
in two worlds, one leg in Lethe,
the other in a leaden Styx, I countered,
but only in my quiet,
the yellow asp stinging the black heart.

27

That was the mind's wild swarm trapezing from an oak limb,
odor of honey and blue sky ablaze—until the regress.
Only what's inmost is left and darkened past language,
and she is like a tiny star that Space no longer notices,
unillumined, hushed, and by herself, her course no longer
in the scheme of planets, suns, and lunar systems.
But she is still here. What breaks the archetypic
stone and starves the honeybees moves toward her slowly.

When bees sicken a rough
leanness or fat mars their appearance: all listless and silent.
Give them honey through straws, freely calling them
and exhorting them to eat their familiar foods
and swallow the Aricept.
But if they fail, may as well say prepare
the hide of a bull with thyme and fresh rosemary
so moisture, warming in the softened bone, ferments—
and without feet at first, but soon with whirring wings as well,
more and more try the clear air, until they burst out
like rain pouring from cumulous clouds,
or arrows from twanging bows (bees are the bow string).
Then the queen revives.

2 9

She doesn't see herself in the mirror,
the mind's white rum
spilt, cosmos a thimble:
When we're diminished to this,
when stars are granular,
candying a thimble of
brain cells, how will we
care? I tell her there are two
of us there in
the mirror, two
faces there. She says no,
I see you, I'm not there.
You'll ask if she smiled
or blinked when she said so. No.

30

Fools die every day they live
And in death, as in sleep,
thought no longer clings to earth's
cool granite. There could be
a wild child and a peacock drinking
themselves from a pool
that agitates in gold and rainbow.
There could be a hell of stars.
In daylight, earth's foot
on their necks, minds ravined
by bees, seasons slowing,
the chalk of their bones softening,
hunchbacked, lost,
emotions strewn,
they listen for the roar of death
to take them to one last
brilliant destination—
flame swerve of ten thousand
candles in that big a wind.

Erring   shoe and sour bib
her dress, wild hair, the woman
is following the turning path.
About her, attendants in white
in a parallel world   wait.
One keeps the drug cart.
One writes on palimpsest
of another fretting mind.

They have not brought her
or kept her   from the clamorous
            world to the labyrinth,
whose entrance   is age,
for reprimand though she feels
it, but simply
to give her a place freely   to move

past season and sun and change
inside coded doors   and honeyed
paneling. At the center
is the courtyard for activity.
Tuesdays a piano plays
and all may dance.

It is no more joyous for them
or for the family until
having walked so long among
the turnings, she loses sense
of direction and all trace

of what it was like before.
It is not easy to be free
forever of a wish never
to go back instead to whirl naked
in a bare world.

32

What makes her quiet
 when they hand her a doll?
What is the doll to her? She's no fool
in this old colony
where half can't wipe up
after themselves. She must know
this May morning in the enclosed
courtyard, a tree white-veiled,
there's no return
to a day when mother
takes her first up in arms.

The doll is naked.
She sees that and maybe hears
inside her head someone crooning,
someone else she can't name.
It's hard to ask her. Her hair is loosened,
her blouse food-bedabbled,
and she no longer apprehends
or doesn't mind the murderous stealth
of shade just starting to break
a bough. Now, *now,*
let her rock her doll.

Man-of-War

From the somber deeps horseshoe crabs crawled up on
somber shores:
Man-of-Wars' blue sails drifted downwind
and blue filaments of some biblical clock
floated below: the stinging filaments:
The cored-of-bone and rock-headed came near:
Clouds made wandering shadows:
Sea and grasses mingled::
There was no hell after all
but a lull before it began over::
flesh lying alone: then mating: a little spray of soul:
and the grace of waves, of stars, and remotest isles.

Notes

I. Voyage to Black Point

The epigraphs for part I are by Dante, *The Inferno,* from Canto I, translated by Robert Pinsky (Farrar, Straus and Giroux, 1996); and by Charles Baudelaire, from "Le Voyage," section CXXVI of *Les Fleurs du Mal;* this version is by the author.

"The Poet's Black Drum"
lines 1–2: An invocation to an unnamed dead poet: Virgil, perhaps, or in modern times Elizabeth Bishop, who fished in Florida waters.
line 5: Barbels are on the under-jaw of black drums, which also have teeth down their gullets.
line 6: Drums fan their tails back and forth to keep in position, finding and eating small blue crabs hiding in oyster beds.

"Black Point"
lines 4–5: The narcotic gases rising from a nearby spring and preserved within the oracle's temple; Apollo once took form as a dolphin to swim out to sea and capture a group of sailors, whom he appointed the first priests of his cult in Delphi.
line 8: The reed pipe Pan made from the transformed body of the nymph Syrinx.
line 13: In mythology, the Corycian Cave was near Delphi and sacred to Pan.
line 15: The python slain by Apollo.
lines 17–18: Pan's and Apollo's music.

"Blue Crab"
line 3: Saturn devoured his sons.
line 9: In Madrid's Prado Museum, Goya's painting of Saturn.

"Dolphin"
line 4: Alexander is one of the "tyrants given to blood and plunder" in Canto XXII of Dante's *Inferno.*
lines 8–10: The Coral Sea in summer is infested with box jellyfish, whose tentacles contain neurotoxins. The wounds gall the bare skin, are excruciating, and can kill. On Northern Queensland beaches in Australia, the warning signs are sometimes ignored by tourists.

"Drowned"
line 2: Fishermen in Cedar Key wear white rubber boots; although commercial net fishing was banned in 1994, fishermen still throw nets.
line 10: Odysseus before he embarked for Troy, then took his ten-year homeward journey.

"Egret"
lines 1–6: The egret, fallen to earth, cannot see the fishes below the water's surface; they are like the stars it cannot see now because of the obsessive gazing down. In Canto XVI of the *Inferno,* one of the three men who link their bodies in a wheel says to Dante, "If you escape from this dark sphere / To see the beauty of the stars, and relish / the pleasure then of saying, 'I was there'—Speak word of us to others."

"Low Tide"

line 9: The river between the dark woods and hell's first circle.

"Manatee"

line 1–2: Mistaken for Sirens for their music; falsifiers.

lines 3–11: References to some of the Violent Sins (across Phlegethon River to the Plain of Fire, in the Seventh Circle).

"Man So Bronzed"

line 5: Haephestus, a "maker," so an artist.

line 7: Both Phlegethon and Xanthes Rivers.

"Redfish"

line 1: Elizabeth Bishop told Robert Lowell that the fish in her poem "The Fish" was a Jewfish.

line 3: As noted in the last chapter of *The Old Man and the Sea*.

line 8: Ammonia and meat tenderizer are Florida remedies for catfish wounds, which are very painful.

"Sea Hare"

line 7: The hideous monsters in hell's depths: Geryon, the harpies, and sinner—"our human image so grotesquely reshaped" (Canto XX, etc., from Pinsky's translation).

"Clam"

line 5–6: Johnny Weismuller, in the 1950s television series.

"North Key"

line 5: Timucuan shell mounds.

"Snake Key"

lines 10–11: As told in chapter five of John Muir's *A Thousand Mile Walk to the Gulf*.

"Voyage"

line 10: Geryon, whose tail is quivery and restless with venomous point (Canto XVI).

line 12: The rivers Acheron, Styx, and Phlgethon, in the *Inferno*; or Channel 6, Goose Creek, and Sand Creek between Cedar Key and Black Point.

line 13: *E quindi uscimmo a riveder le stelle* (Canto XXXIV, line 140).

II. Abstractions

The epigraphs for part II are by Charles Baudelaire, from "Salon of 1846," section 18 of *Curiosités Esthétiques* (1868), included in *The Mirror of Art*, edited by Jonathan Mayne (Phaidon, 1955); and by Rainer Maria Rilke, from "For Hans Carossa," translated by Edward Snow, included in *Uncollected Poems* (North Point Press, 1996).

"Her Beauty"

line 6: In the story of Psyche and Cupid, Cupid's mother Venus, goddess of love, becomes jealous of Psyche because of the mortal girl's beauty.

"Homo sapiens"

lines 8–9: At what moment in evolution did individuals in the group begin to think of themselves as other than animal?

"Horror"

line 6: Goya's "Black Paintings," first painted on the walls of his house, were transferred onto canvas fifty years after his death and are now exhibited at the Prado Museum in Madrid.

line 7: Untitled by Goya, the painting of the dog is known colloquially as "Goya's Dog" and by the Spanish names *"Perro"* and *"Perro Semihundido."*

"Laws"

line 11: Exodus 34:28.

"The Past"

line 2: The Martin homestead, on Otsdawa Creek Road, in Otego, New York.

"Pure"

line 1: On November 26, 1991, the *New York Times* reported the event of a father accidentally shooting his son while they were hunting.

"Soul"

line 2: George Segal's plaster casts from live models.

"Wilderness"

line 1: William Bartram, 18th-century naturalist.

line 3: The John Muir phrase is from "The American Forests," published in *The Atlantic,* August 1, 1897. John James Audubon shot the birds he drew and painted.

line 8: Arcturus, in the constellation Boötes, is the brightest star in the northern celestial hemisphere.

III. The Apiary Poems

The epigraph for part III is by Pliny the Elder, from *The Natural History,* chapter 12, "The Qualities of Honey," edited by John Bostock and H. T. Riley (G. Bell & Sons, six volumes: 1856–1893). Available online at: www.perseus.tufts.edu/hopper/text?doc=Perseus:text:1999.02.01374

"(Tyrannus, tyrannus)..."

line 1: The Eastern kingbird is a large tyrant flycatcher, from the flycatcher family *Tyrannidae.*

5 "I remember..."

line 2: Drawing a clock by hand is one of several screening tools that can help to detect mild cognitive impairment, dementia, or Alzheimer's.

7 "Two anthills . . ."

line 19: Bee bread is the mixture of collected pollen and nectar or honey, deposited in the cells to feed young bees.

line 33: The English translation for *"Wer bist du"* is "Who are you."

11 "Amid a menagerie . . ."

line 7: Judges 14:8.

13 "It was August . . ."

line 13: "Embrace me, my sweet embraceable you."

19 "The mind is no tunnel . . ."

line 7: Title of poem by the German poet Heinrich Heine.

21 "Light clear . . ."

line 10: Opera house in Vienna, Austria.

line 17: Orpheus myth.

line 21: A German actor and singer.

23 "The humble sense . . ."

line 5: Greek goddess of memory and remembrance, and of words and language; mother of the nine muses.

26 "When bees sicken . . ."

Parts of the poem are adapted from Virgil's *Georgics,* Book IV, lines 251–280, translated by A. S. Kline.

Other books from Tupelo Press

Fasting for Ramadan: Notes from a Spiritual Practice (memoir), Kazim Ali
Moonbook and Sunbook (poems), Willis Barnstone
Another English: Anglophone Poems from Around the World (anthology),
    edited by Catherine Barnett and Tiphanie Yanique
Circle's Apprentice (poems), Dan Beachy-Quick
The Vital System (poems), CM Burroughs
Stone Lyre: Poems of René Char, translated by Nancy Naomi Carlson
Living Wages (poems), Michael Chitwood
Severance Songs (poems), Joshua Corey
Atlas Hour (poems), Carol Ann Davis
New Cathay: Contemporary Chinese Poetry (anthology), edited by Ming Di
Sanderlings (poems), Geri Doran
The Flight Cage (poems), Rebecca Dunham
The Posthumous Affair (novel), James Friel
Into Daylight (poems), Jeffrey Harrison
Ay (poems), Joan Houlihan
The Faulkes Chronicle (novel), David Huddle
Darktown Follies (poems), Amaud Jamaul Johnson
Dancing in Odessa (poems), Ilya Kaminsky
A God in the House: Poets Talk About Faith (interviews),
    edited by Ilya Kaminsky and Katherine Towler
domina Un/blued (poems), Ruth Ellen Kocher
Phyla of Joy (poems), Karen An-hwei Lee
Boat (poems), Christopher Merrill
Lucky Fish (poems), Aimee Nezhukumatathil
Long Division (poems), Alan Michael Parker
Ex-Voto (poems), Adélia Prado, translated by Ellen Doré Watson
Intimate: An American Family Photo Album (memoir), Paisley Rekdal
Thrill-Bent (novel), Jan Richman
Calendars of Fire (poems), Lee Sharkey
Cream of Kohlrabi: Stories, Floyd Skloot
The Perfect Life (essays), Peter Stitt
Swallowing the Sea (essays), Lee Upton
Butch Geography (poems), Stacey Waite
Dogged Hearts (poems), Ellen Doré Watson

See our complete backlist at www.tupelopress.org